Biography.

John GLENN

Tom Streissguth

Lerner Publications Company
Minneapolis

This book is available in two bindings:
Library binding by Lerner Publications Company
Softcover by First Avenue Editions
Divisions of the Lerner Publishing Group
241 First Avenue North
Minneapolis, MN 55401

Website address: www.lernerbooks.com

Library of Congress Cataloging-in-Publication Data

Streissguth, Thomas, 1958–
   John Glenn / Tom Streissguth.
       p.   cm.
   Includes bibliographical references and index.
   Summary: Describes the life of John Glenn, including his childhood, World War II activities, work as a test pilot and astronaut, career as a senator, and return to space in 1998.
   ISBN 0-8225-4947-6 (alk. paper)
   ISBN 0-8225-9685-7 (pbk. : alk. paper)
   1. Glenn, John, 1921– —Juvenile literature. 2. Legislators—United States—Biography—Juvenile literature. 3. Astronauts—United States—Biography—Juvenile literature. 4. United States. Congress. House—Biography—Juvenile literature. [1. Glenn, John, 1921– . 2. Legislators. 3. Astronauts.] I. Title.
   E840.8.G54S77 1999
   973.92'092—dc21
   [B]   99-10832

Manufactured in the United States of America
1 2 3 4 5 6 – JR – 04 03 02 01 00 99

CONTENTS

Major John Glenn, standing next to the bullet-ridden hull of his plane

Chapter **ONE**

LEARNING TO FLY

ON JULY 18, 1921, JOHN HERSCHEL GLENN JR. was born in Cambridge, a town in the rolling hills of southeastern Ohio. When John was still a young boy, his parents moved to the nearby town of New Concord. Both towns lie along the old National Road, the route that brought many nineteenth-century immigrants westward into the Ohio River valley and the Midwest. New Concord's founders were Presbyterians—strict, religious people from England and Scotland—who believed in hard work and the bonds of family and community. In the 1920s, most of the people of New Concord still held those beliefs, which also strongly influenced John.

The Glenn family had a long, proud military history.

John Glenn's parents standing in front of his boyhood home in New Concord, Ohio

Two of John Glenn's great-grandfathers had fought on the side of the Union during the Civil War. John's father had fought in France during World War I, and his hearing had been impaired as a result of the fighting. After the war, John Glenn Sr. started a plumbing business and managed to make a comfortable living for himself and his family.

John's mother, Clara Sproat Glenn, was strong-willed, outgoing, and extremely devout. Although she wanted a large family, two of her children died while they were infants. After John was born, the family adopted a young girl named Jean. Clara told her children that each person is placed on Earth for a purpose. Her strong sense of mission and duty influenced John throughout his life.

Although John Glenn's family was strict, he enjoyed a happy and carefree boyhood. He played stickball and hockey in the streets and rambled in the surrounding fields. He excelled in sports by making up in determination what he lacked in speed, strength, and natural athletic talent. His parents and teachers could tell that he was a natural leader. New Concord was still too small to organize its own Boy Scout troop, so John started a group of his own, calling it the Ohio Rangers.

Airplanes and flight fascinated John more than anything else. He read all the aviation books he could find and built small wooden models in his room. His boyhood hero was Charles Lindbergh, who in 1927 became the first person to fly solo across the Atlantic Ocean. One day a family friend invited John and his father to join him for a short airplane ride. The flight thrilled John, who afterward decided on a future career as a pilot.

Charles Lindbergh and the Spirit of St. Louis

John Glenn was a member of the New Concord Varsity Club. He is in the front row, fourth from the left.

In the 1930s, a worldwide business slump that became known as the Great Depression hit the United States—including the town of New Concord. Many people lost their jobs at the local mills and coal mines and could no longer afford to buy even basic necessities. John Glenn Sr.'s plumbing business also suffered. Although the Glenn family always had enough to eat, John saw many other people go hungry and even lose their homes.

When President Franklin D. Roosevelt began programs to help people find work, John realized that politicians could do more than just campaign for election. The Glenn family remained in the Democratic Party—Roosevelt's party—while most other people in conservative New Concord voted Republican.

In 1935, just as the country was beginning to pull out of the Depression, John entered New Concord High School. He earned high marks in his classes and lettered in football, basketball, and tennis. John stud-

John, as a high school senior, and Annie, as a college sophomore

ied American government with a teacher named Harford Steele. Mr. Steele was very strict, but he inspired John with an interest in American history and the U.S. Congress. In a sense, John began his political career when students at New Concord elected him president of the junior class.

When he was still a little boy, John had made friends with Annie Castor, the daughter of a New Concord dentist. While the two attended high school, Annie became John's sweetheart. After finishing high school, John and Annie both stayed in New Concord to attend Muskingum College, which John entered in the fall of 1939. Reflecting the spirit of the town, Muskingum strictly controlled the behavior of its students. Driving cars was forbidden—as was smoking, drinking, and staying out past the evening curfew. John made the football squad, was a member of the

The serene Muskingum College campus

Varsity Club, did well in his classes, and never had a problem with the rules.

Although New Concord remained isolated and quiet during the 1930s, trouble was brewing in other parts of the world. Under the leadership of Adolf Hitler, Germany was strengthening its army and its arsenals and invading the neighboring countries of Austria and Czechoslovakia. In 1939, when Hitler ordered the invasion of Poland, World War II began.

At the outbreak of the war, the United States remained neutral, although it was closely allied with Great Britain, France, and the other nations at war with Germany. Along with many other people, Glenn believed that the United States would eventually be drawn into the war. Civilian pilot training programs expanded throughout the country. John Glenn volunteered for a program at New Philadelphia, a nearby airfield. Although he had to wait a year, Glenn entered the program in 1940 and learned the basics of aerodynamics, takeoffs and landings, and instrument flying. He completed the program and earned his first private pilot's license in July 1941.

Later that year, on December 7, Germany's ally Japan attacked Pearl Harbor, Hawaii, an important U.S. military base in the Pacific Ocean. The next day, President Roosevelt declared war on Japan. On December 11, Germany and Italy declared war on the United States. John Glenn decided to follow in the footsteps of his father and great-grandfathers by defending his country. Glenn dropped out of college, enlisted in the Navy Air Corps, and was assigned to a naval air base in Corpus Christi, Texas.

Major John Glenn beside the plane he flew during the Korean War

Chapter **TWO**

FIGHTING IN THE AIR

THE **UNITED STATES MILITARY HAD STARTED USING** airplanes during World War I. While the infantry fought in trenches in the northern plains of France, pilots flew small planes fitted with machine guns for aerial fighting or stocked with bombs for attacking enemy troops on the ground. Airplanes also proved extremely useful in reconnaissance work. From the air, pilots could spot enemy troop formations and movements, locate supply depots, and direct artillery bombardments. By the outbreak of World War II, all the nations involved had built up their air forces, knowing that control of the air would be crucial to victory.

When John Glenn reported to the Corpus Christi Naval Air Station in early 1942, however, the United

States did not have a separate air force. Each branch of the service ran its own air operation. Although the largest was the Army Air Corps, the Navy and the Marine Corps had their own smaller air forces.

Each branch of the service also had its own bases for training fighter and bomber pilots. The Corpus Christi Naval Air Station was located in Texas, along the flat, sandy coast of the Gulf of Mexico. During World War II, more than twenty thousand pilots trained there.

Glenn began his own navy flight training in PBY seaplanes, designed to take off and land on water as well as dry ground. He practiced flying the planes, took classes in navigation and airborne weaponry, and patrolled the Gulf of Mexico for enemy submarines.

Glenn's ability and determination earned him high marks and praise from his superiors at Corpus Christi. After he finished training, Glenn graduated as a lieutenant and was notified that he qualified for enlistment in the Marine Corps. Although he felt uncertain about a military career, a recruiter's remark that Glenn probably wasn't good enough for the Marine Corps goaded him into signing up.

On April 6, 1943, John married Anna Margaret Castor. A reception at the bride's home followed an informal ceremony. A wedding photograph shows John in his Marine uniform and Annie in a frilly white dress.

Glenn's first Marine Corps assignment was to Cherry Point, North Carolina, where he looked forward to further training in combat planes—fighters and bombers.

But at this early stage in the war, the Marines had many more pilots than planes, and for long stretches Glenn got very little flying time. For a military pilot, flight time was the single most important measure of success and advancement. More hours in the air meant better preparation for the day when the pilot would have to move overseas and face the enemy. Also, to earn "flight pay" in addition to the meager military salary, a pilot had to fly at least four hours each month.

From Cherry Point, Glenn was transferred to Camp Kearney, California, where he was assigned to fly transport planes. From there, he was moved to El Centro Air Station in California. There he trained in fighter planes—first 4F4 Wildcats and then Corsairs, huge planes with massive engines.

In February 1944, more than two years after the United States entered the war, Glenn was shipped out on the cargo ship *Santa Monica* to Midway Island in the Pacific Ocean. This small island, located at the northwestern edge of the Hawaiian Islands, served as a U.S. air and submarine base. In June 1942, Midway had been the site of a huge naval battle, the first in history in which air power and aircraft carriers had played the most important role in the outcome. The United States had won the battle, sinking four Japanese carriers and ending Japan's threat to Midway and the Hawaiian Islands.

During the spring of 1944, Glenn flew patrol missions in the area, keeping a lookout for Japanese ships, planes, and submarines. That summer, he saw his first fighting in the Marshall Islands, located in the central Pacific Ocean. After suffering heavy losses while trying to defeat the Japanese on the ground, U.S. commanders decided instead to bomb the enemy off the islands. Glenn flew dozens of bombing missions in Corsairs, attacking infantry and antiaircraft positions. He flew fast and low to avoid antiaircraft barrages at higher altitudes.

On August 6 and August 9, 1945, the United States dropped atomic bombs on the Japanese cities of Hiroshima and Nagasaki. On August 14, the war in the Pacific finally ended. At that point, John Glenn had some important decisions to make. He could retire from the military and return to Annie and his parents in New Concord. (His father looked forward to turn-

U.S. Marines rest in a foxhole soon after landing on Namur Beach in the Marshall Islands.

UNION OF THE SOVIET
SOCIALIST
REPUBLIC (USSR)

MANCHURIA

Beijing

KOREA

CHINA

Tokyo

JAPAN

Hiroshima

Nagasaki

Okinawa

PHILIPPINE
ISLANDS

Guam

PACIFIC OCEAN

Battle of Midway,
June 1942

Midway
Island

Pearl Harbor,
Dec. 7, 1941

Hawaiian
Islands

Marshall
Islands

Guadalcanal

**World War II in Asia
and the Pacific**

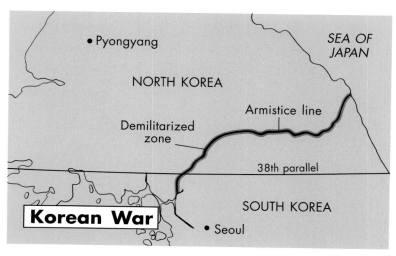

Pyongyang

SEA OF
JAPAN

NORTH KOREA

Armistice line

Demilitarized
zone

38th parallel

SOUTH KOREA

Korean War

Seoul

ing over a successful plumbing business to John.) But since he had had a good stint as a military flier, Glenn had other options as well. He could fulfill his boyhood dream of becoming a commercial airline pilot—or he could make the Marine Corps his career.

Glenn decided that he did not want to leave the excitement of military flying behind him. He knew that even during peacetime, skilled pilots would be needed to test-fly new planes. Glenn looked forward to the challenge and accepted an offer to stay in the Marine Corps.

The decision was not an easy one, however, since Glenn had a growing family. In 1945, Annie had given birth to a son named David. On March 15, 1947, while John was stationed in Okinawa, an island in the distant seas near Japan and China, Annie gave birth again—this time to a daughter named Carolyn, usually called Lyn. Although the birth itself went well, Annie contracted an infection and a life-threatening fever soon after she returned home. Her parents rushed her back to the hospital.

When John learned about Annie's condition, he got emergency medical leave and flew home. The trip from his base took three days, however. By the time John arrived at the hospital, Annie was too sick to recognize him.

Eventually the medicine took effect and Annie recovered. Glenn returned to Okinawa and later moved to the island of Guam, which served as a U.S. air and naval base in the Pacific Ocean. Soon, Glenn's family joined him. By this time, Annie had grown more accustomed to the life of worry and uncertainty that military wives experienced. She was learning to accept the frequent moves, and she supported her husband's decisions and ambitions.

After the war, Glenn rose in the ranks from lieutenant to captain to major. He continued to fly at bases in Maryland, California, and the Pacific. At one point, he was assigned to Fighter Squadron 218 in northern China. While a civil war raged between the Communist and Nationalist Chinese armies, Glenn flew air patrols.

The civil war in China was considered part of the worldwide "Cold War" that had developed between Communist and non-Communist nations after World War II. The struggle was called the Cold War because it did not lead to actual fighting on a wide scale. The United States and the Soviet Union and their allies formed two blocs. Each wanted to impose its vision on the world. The United States wanted a world of independent nations based on democracy and open markets. The Soviet Union wanted tight control of the government and large segments of the economy in regions it considered vital to its national interest. The clash between these two systems of government overshadowed the civil war in China, which the Communists eventually won. The Cold War was also a factor behind the fighting in Korea, where a group allied to the

Communist Chinese fought to overthrow the South Korean government.

In 1950, the United States found itself drawn directly into the Korean conflict. Communist forces in the north had invaded much of South Korea and were threatening to overrun the country completely. To avoid this outcome, the United Nations, an international organization established in 1945 to work for world peace and security, sent ground troops into Korea in 1950. Troops from the United States made up the largest part of this international military force.

The Korean War dragged on for several years without an outcome. In the meantime, Glenn served as flight instructor at Corpus Christi and took a course in amphibious warfare at the Marine base in Quantico, Virginia. In February 1953, John Glenn was sent to Korea to join Marine Corps Fighter Squadron 311 at a

Sabrejets were used to bomb North Korea during the Korean War.

base in Pohang Dong Ni. The squadron flew F9F Pantherjets—jet fighters that could carry heavy bombs as well as machine guns for air combat. Glenn ably flew several dozen bombing missions over Korea. Eager for one-on-one combat, he later arranged to have himself transferred to an Air Force squadron flying F86 Sabrejet fighter planes. On July 12, 1953, Glenn scored his first victory in aerial dogfights by downing a MiG fighter, a plane manufactured by the Soviet Union. He shot down two more MiGs within the next two weeks before the war was ended by a cease-fire on July 27, 1953.

During World War II and the Korean War, Glenn had flown a total of 149 missions. He had survived antiaircraft fire and one-on-one air combat without injury and had been awarded five Distinguished Flying Crosses for his skill.

Glenn was the first person to fly across the United States faster than the speed of sound.

Chapter **THREE**

PUSHING THE ENVELOPE

DURING THE KOREAN WAR, GLENN HAD FLOWN the fastest, most advanced fighter planes the United States had in its arsenal. But hostilities had ended and peacetime had come. Like many other military pilots, Glenn realized the best way to get ahead and continue flying was to become a test pilot. He applied for assignment to the Patuxent River Naval Air Station, nicknamed "Pax River," in Maryland. At the air station, former combat pilots faced a tough academic and flight-training program designed to graduate professional test pilots.

Although Glenn had served with distinction in Korea, he had to convince the officers at Pax River that he could qualify for their program. He asked two of his former commanders in Korea to endorse him. Glenn was accepted, but the program demanded advanced math skills and a basic knowledge of calculus, which Glenn had not studied in his two years at Muskingum College. He mustered the determination that had helped him before, however, and managed to master the math and graduate from Pax River as a marine test pilot in August 1954.

Test pilots at Pax River and at Edwards Air Force base in California were flying higher and faster than ever before. On October 14, 1947, Captain Chuck Yaeger had been the first human to fly faster than the speed of sound. Yaeger had accomplished this feat in the X-1, a rocket plane that was fueled by alcohol and liquid oxygen cooled to a temperature of minus 297 degrees Fahrenheit. After proving that the sound barrier could be broken, the Air Force designed the first supersonic fighter, the F-100 Super Sabre, and a supersonic bomber, the B-58 Hustler.

At Pax River, Glenn began to work in a new fighter known as the F8U Crusader. The job of test pilots was to "push the envelope," in other words, to take risks. They had to push the planes as high and as fast as they could go, find out how well they maneuvered at high speeds, and determine at what speed they would stall or lose the aerodynamics that kept them in the air. It was dangerous and demanding work. Dozens of test pilots died in fiery crashes. Others simply lost their nerve after enough close calls.

For two years, Glenn flew the Crusader and other supersonic aircraft with no accidents or damage to his planes or himself. In 1956, however, he was transferred to a desk job at the Bureau of Naval Aeronautics in Washington, D.C., where he worked in the Fighter Design Branch. Although he had a safer job that might lead to more promotions, Glenn missed test flying, and he was still seeking ways to advance his career as a military pilot.

At the Bureau of Naval Aeronautics, Glenn learned about a project that would take a jet plane from coast to coast at top speeds. Using his political skills, persistence, and persuasion, Glenn managed to get himself assigned to the project as the pilot. He worked out a flight plan for what he nicknamed Operation Bullet and made preparations for takeoff, landing, and midair refueling. Taking off from Los Alamitos Naval Air Station in California on July 16, 1957, Glenn flew a Crusader to an altitude of 50,000 feet, almost ten miles high. He followed a course that took him east and north, directly over his hometown of New Concord. The Crusader reached speeds of more than 1,000 miles per hour—one and a half times the speed of sound. Three times during the flight, the Crusader slowed and descended to 25,000 feet to refuel. Three hours, 23 minutes, and 8.4 seconds after takeoff, Glenn landed at Bennett Field in Brooklyn, New York, setting a new transcontinental speed record. Annie, Dave, and Lyn were there to greet him.

Glenn is greeted by his wife, Annie, and his children, David and Lyn, after his record-breaking flight.

Overnight, Operation Bullet turned John Glenn from an unknown test pilot into an aviation hero. Glenn embarked on a speaking tour and saw himself written up in newspapers and magazines. His straightforward patriotism and enthusiasm went over well among audiences. The country saw Operation Bullet as a deed of heroism and as an important scientific and military achievement.

Such achievements had begun to replace battlefield victories as a measure of success during the Cold War. The United States and the Soviet Union were building new planes, tanks, ships, and weapons—including nuclear weapons—that threatened not just defeat to the enemy in wartime but the destruction of the planet

Secretary of the Navy Thomas Gates pins the Distinguished Flying Cross on Glenn.

and civilization itself. Glenn realized the stakes were high, and events that showed the daring and know-how of the United States were essential in the new international competition.

The most crucial scientific battle fought during the Cold War was the "race for space." Both sides knew that some day, vessels would be designed to fly above the Earth's atmosphere in space. Both sides also explored the possibility of launching nuclear weapons from space. To prepare for this, the U.S. military designed and built rockets—including the Jupiter, the Viking, and the Redstone—that would someday be capable of carrying weapons above the atmosphere.

The U.S. Air Force designed the X-15B, a winged aircraft powered by three rocket engines. The X-15B was designed to fly in orbit around the Earth with two pilots aboard. The pilots would be able to control the flight path, altitude, and speed of the plane. Plans called for a rocket booster to lift the X-15B from the ground. The booster would then fall away, and the plane would orbit the Earth several times before returning to a normal aircraft runway.

By the fall of 1957, however, the booster vehicle had not yet been built, and the orbital flights of the X-15B were still in their planning stages. Then on October 4, the Soviet Union launched *Sputnik*, the first artificial satellite, into space. *Sputnik* was about the size of a beach ball and was only capable of simple radio communication from space. Nevertheless, the successful launch put the Soviets ahead in the space race.

Just two months later, the Soviets launched *Sputnik II*, a much larger satellite that carried a small dog named Laika as a passenger. The satellite flew several orbits around the Earth before returning, thus proving that an Earthbound organism could survive for an extended period of time in space. (Laika, however, died during reentry.)

For most Americans, *Sputnik* represented not just a scientific achievement but also a military threat, because it meant the Soviets might have the capability to attack from space. Many officials believed that the country needed a demonstration of U.S. rocket and satellite technology immediately. On December 6, 1957, a ground crew moved a Vanguard rocket with a small satellite aboard to a launching pad at Cape Canaveral, on the Atlantic coast of Florida. A tense countdown began. At zero, the rocket lifted a few inches from its launching pad, stalled, fell back to the ground, and exploded.

The failure of the first Vanguard liftoff almost threw the United States into a nationwide panic. In a famous speech, Senator Lyndon Johnson of Texas, then the Senate Majority Leader, described control of space as a means to world domination. In another speech, Congressman John McCormack of Massachusetts, then Speaker of the House of Representatives, declared that ". . . the survival of the Free World—indeed all the world—is caught up in these stakes."

With public and political pressure mounting, the military gave the space program top priority. In 1958, the National Aeronautics and Space Administration (NASA) was established to plan space missions; build launch vehicles, satellites, and crewed spacecraft; and recruit scientists, engineers, and astronauts. Instead of pursuing the undeveloped X-15B planes, NASA officials decided to build a capsule that would be launched into the sky like a bullet, circle the Earth at the speed and altitude needed to stay in orbit, and then return under the control of retro rockets and parachutes. Rocket boosters that had already been built, including the U.S. Army's Redstone and the much larger but untested Atlas rocket, would be used.

NASA set a goal to put a man in space by the middle of 1960. The agency dubbed its crewed program "Mercury," after the fleet-footed god of roads and travel in ancient Roman mythology. The nation's future astronauts would be selected from the 540 military test pilots who were already flying at Pax

River, Edwards Air Force Base, and other test-flight centers. The candidates could be no older than thirty-nine and no taller than five feet eleven inches. They had to have at least fifteen hundred hours of flight time, and they had to have a bachelor's degree—a requirement that disqualified Chuck Yaeger, the nation's most skilled test pilot.

The test pilots soon learned that the astronauts would not necessarily have to be good at flying. As writer Tom Wolfe described it, the Project Mercury astronaut "would be a human cannonball. He would not be able to alter the course of the capsule in the slightest. The capsule would go up like a cannonball and come down like a cannonball, splashing into the ocean, with a parachute to slow it down and spare the life of the human specimen inside."

NASA's first astronauts would be used almost as lab animals. They would be shot into space so scientists on Earth could discover the effects of weightlessness and spaceflight on the human body. Although they would not actually be piloting the spacecraft, many test pilots volunteered for the program, seeing it as a way to advance their careers and improve their ranks. Major John Glenn, one of the first and most eager of the volunteers, had heard about the program while working at the Bureau of Naval Aeronautics in Washington, D.C.

GETTING INTO SPACE

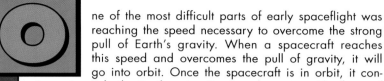

ne of the most difficult parts of early spaceflight was reaching the speed necessary to overcome the strong pull of Earth's gravity. When a spacecraft reaches this speed and overcomes the pull of gravity, it will go into orbit. Once the spacecraft is in orbit, it continues to circle the Earth, using its own momentum. The force of gravity keeps it from floating away into outer space. Rockets, such as the Redstone and the *Atlas,* provided thrust to the *Mercury* capsules.

To return to Earth, the craft must be able to slow down. This job was assigned to the astronaut and the *retro rockets.* By firing retro rockets in the same direction the spacecraft is flying, the astronaut slows the speed of the spacecraft and it begins to fall back toward Earth under the force of gravity.

When the spacecraft reenters the atmosphere, the astronaut must be careful. If the craft is pointing straight down, friction will burn it up. If the craft is not pointing toward the Earth, it will skip off the atmosphere and continue in its orbit or out of Earth's gravity field into outer space. Once the craft reaches close enough to Earth, the astronaut slows it down even further by firing parachutes, which allow the craft to land without damage.

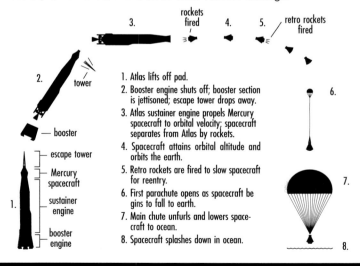

1. Atlas lifts off pad.
2. Booster engine shuts off; booster section is jettisoned; escape tower drops away.
3. Atlas sustainer engine propels Mercury spacecraft to orbital velocity; spacecraft separates from Atlas by rockets.
4. Spacecraft attains orbital altitude and orbits the earth.
5. Retro rockets are fired to slow spacecraft for reentry.
6. First parachute opens as spacecraft begins to fall to earth.
7. Main chute unfurls and lowers spacecraft to ocean.
8. Spacecraft splashes down in ocean.

Mercury Redstone III blasting off

Chapter **FOUR**

GETTING WITH THE PROGRAM

GLENN **REALIZED HE WOULD HAVE PROBLEMS** qualifying for the Mercury program. He was thirty-eight years old—still young enough, but probably older than most of the other candidates. He was also six feet tall, and he had a stocky build that might make him too heavy for the Mercury capsule. He did have enough flying time and test pilot experience—but like Chuck Yaeger, he still did not have a college degree.

With his usual determination, Glenn tried to push the process forward anyway. He put himself through exhausting physical workouts to get his weight down. He spent hours walking around with a stack of books on his head, trying to shrink himself to the necessary height limit. He also asked for recommendations from old commanding officers, including Colonel Jake Dill at Pax River. Determined to see that at least one Marine flier made the program, Dill went directly to NASA headquarters to insist that Glenn be accepted.

The educational hurdle would not be so easy to overcome, however. Glenn had spent only two years at Muskingum College, but he had also spent a year in an intensive study of aeronautics and mathematics at Pax River. Impressed by his background and his stubbornness, NASA decided to accept Glenn, along with 109 other volunteers as Mercury candidates.

NASA officials spent many hours interviewing each candidate and explaining the Mercury program in detail. Each pilot had to answer hundreds of questions about his personal life, his military background, his flying experience, and his attitude toward risk and danger. The pilots also had to think about how the Mercury program would affect their careers. Many fliers still believed that *piloted* rocket planes, such as the X-15B, would ultimately serve as space exploration vehicles. The small, cone-shaped Mercury spacecraft looked more like a big can made out of corrugated steel. If the pilots joined the Mercury program, they would be strapped into the tiny capsule while missing out on future X-15 flights and any promotions that might come with them. Only physical endurance would be required of Mercury astronauts. They would fly the capsule only if the engine and navigation controls failed in some way.

Glenn, third from left, *showed a natural talent for dealing with reporters.*

If the Mercury program did fail, lives as well as careers would be in jeopardy—but the program did have the full backing of the government and the military. The first and most important goal was to put a man in space before the Soviets, and Mercury was the fastest way of doing so. If the program succeeded and the astronauts survived the flights, they would become national heroes.

NASA split the finalists into five groups of six and one group of two, then moved them to the Lovelace Clinic in Albuquerque, New Mexico. There, a team of doctors put the candidates through a weeklong series of physical tests and ordeals, including blood tests, urinalysis, X rays, enemas, strength and reflex tests, and sperm counts. When asked, the doctors never explained the purpose of these tests. In fact, NASA's doctors were not too concerned with physical conditioning, which they knew would be excellent in all the candidates. Instead, they wanted to find out how much pain the pilots could stand and how well they might perform as human guinea pigs in space. The Lovelace Clinic proved to be the end of the road for many Mercury candidates, several of whom quit in frustration and anger.

To measure the candidates' ability to withstand the unique stress of spaceflight, Glenn and the other finalists went to Wright-Patterson Air Force Base, near Dayton, Ohio. There they were given another series of intense tests. The astronaut candidates were placed in spaceflight simulators that created the heavy vibrations, turbulence, and high "g forces" expected during the Mercury flights. (One g is equal to the force of gravity on the body at rest. Increasing g forces are experienced during rapid speed changes, which put great pressure on the body.) The candidates had to withstand extreme heat and cold, deafening noises, and long periods of lying flat on their backs—the position they would have to assume inside the Mercury capsule. To test their nerves, they also were put in a dark room and deprived of all light and sound for several hours.

One of the candidates, Donald "Deke" Slayton, wrote: "While I thought the Lovelace physical examinations were excessive, I could at least see the point. But the idea behind all these so-called "stress" tests at Wright-Patterson escaped me completely. . . ."

Nevertheless, the testing went on for months. Finally, on April 9, 1959, NASA held a press conference to announce the final cut—the roster of seven men who would be the first Americans to fly into space and orbit the Earth. Wally Schirra, Scott Carpenter, Alan Shepard, Gus Grissom, Deke Slayton, Gordon Cooper, and John Glenn sat behind a long table and faced members of the media.

While photographers snapped pictures, reporters asked the astronauts many questions, most of them silly or repetitive, about the risks of spaceflight, fear of accidents and dying, and wives and home life. Although each man gave answers, several grew uncomfortable with the questions. They were not used to reporters prying into their private lives and feelings, and they felt overwhelmed by the sudden publicity. The one exception was John Glenn.

Glenn had no problem dealing with reporters or putting together quotable phrases for the media. In his memoirs, Deke Slayton remembers that "...the real surprise was watching John Glenn. He ate this stuff up. Somebody asked if our wives were behind us. Six of us said 'Sure,' as if that had ever been a real consideration. Glenn piped up with a damn speech about God and family and destiny. We all looked at him, then at each other." Glenn's ease with reporters and with the public spotlight soon made him an unofficial leader of the group. Reporters knew they could always depend on him for a good quote.

Most reporters would not have many more chances

NASA introduces the first U.S. astronauts. From left to right, Scott Carpenter, Gordon Cooper, John Glenn, Virgil Grissom, Walter Schirra, Alan Shepard, and Donald Slayton.

to speak with Glenn or any of the other members of the "Mercury Seven" about their personal lives, however. NASA knew that the sudden public attention would attract a crowd of pesky writers demanding stories, gossip, and information. For this reason, NASA decided to sell the rights to the astronauts' stories to a single bidder.

Serving as the astronauts' agent, a New York lawyer named Leo DeOrsey sold the rights to *Life* magazine for $500,000. The money would be split evenly among the seven astronauts over a period of four years. In return, the magazine was granted exclusive access to the astronauts for information about their personal lives. The seven astronauts could discuss details of the Mercury flights with anyone, but they could not reveal their home and personal life to any publication except *Life*. The magazine ran a series of biographical articles under the astronauts' bylines, but the stories were actually written by magazine staffers. The stories were always positive and supportive, giving the public an image of hard-working, clean-cut heroes who cheerfully risked their lives for the sake of science and the

Glenn at a training operation at Langley Field, Virginia. Some of the Mercury capsule's controls are visible through the windows.

race for space. Although the arrangement caused bitterness among *Life's* many competitors, it did relieve some of the publicity pressure placed on the astronauts, and it helped them out financially.

The Mercury Seven moved to the vicinity of Langley Air Force Base in Virginia, where NASA had set up its headquarters. From this base, the group spent long periods traveling around the country, getting familiar with the different components of the Mercury program. In St. Louis, Missouri, they inspected the Mercury capsules that were under construction at a McDonnell Aircraft Corporation plant; at Cape Canaveral, they toured the launching facilities; in Huntsville, Alabama, they saw the Redstone rockets; at a Corsair plant in San Diego, they inspected Atlas rockets.

There were thousands of details to master and problems to overcome. No single astronaut could cover them all, so each man was assigned a particular area of the Mercury flights. Deke Slayton was in charge of the Atlas rocket, while Gordon Cooper was assigned the Redstone. Wally Schirra was assigned pressure suits. Al Shepard researched the problems of tracking the capsule from the ground and recovering it from the sea. Scott Carpenter handled navigation and radio communications, and Gus Grissom studied the manual and automatic capsule thrusters. John Glenn's realm was the interior design of the spacecraft itself— the controls, switches, and gauges to be used by the astronauts in flight.

NASA was eager for launches to begin as soon as possible. The agency planned to make a series of suborbital flights on a Redstone rocket in early 1960. These flights would take the spacecraft up to a certain altitude, but not high enough to orbit the Earth. Then NASA would switch to orbital flights, during which the capsule would circle the Earth one or more times.

NASA had scheduled the program to finish by the end of 1961, but technical problems delayed it. The Atlas rocket failed on four out of every ten test launches, and tests of a dummy Mercury capsule—one with no astronaut and hardly any instruments—were also unsuccessful. On July 29, 1960, a countdown began at Cape Canaveral for the launch of Mercury-Atlas 1. As the first Mercury flight to carry a number, this launch signaled the end of the long period of testing and experimentation, and the beginning of the program's official flights. This was to be the first Atlas rocket to carry a complete Mercury capsule, and the best simulation yet of the conditions of a crewed spaceflight. One minute after the launch, at an altitude of 32,000 feet, the Atlas exploded.

While NASA was trying to solve the problems with the Atlas, Glenn and the other astronauts went through more tough physical training. They trained in spaceflight simulators and pressure chambers to simulate high altitudes. They learned underwater diving in preparation for the splashdowns on the return flight, and they underwent desert survival training, because the Mercury orbital flights would cross the Sahara Desert in Africa. They also flew on C-47 planes at Holloman Air Force Base in New Mexico. Pilots flew the planes in high arcs during which the astronauts experienced a few seconds of weightlessness.

In the fall of 1960, John F. Kennedy was elected president. By this time, the public knew NASA more for its failures and delays than for space exploration, and the Soviet space program was still more advanced and successful than its U.S. counterpart. Worried that Kennedy might decide to cancel the troubled Mercury program, NASA decided to push ahead quickly with more tests. Officials at NASA also wanted to select an astronaut for the first flight, which would be a short, suborbital flight using a Redstone rocket.

Bob Gilruth, the director of the Space Task Group that was selecting and training the Mercury astronauts, decided to hold a peer vote among the Mercury Seven. Each astronaut had to vote for the best man to take the first flight, if he couldn't make the flight himself. As Tom Wolfe explains, "Peer votes were not unknown in the military... but peer votes had never amounted to anything more than... an indication of how men at the same level regarded one another, whether for reasons of professionalism or friendship or jealousy or whatever. Pilots regarded peer votes as a waste of time, because a man either had the right stuff in the air or he didn't, and a military career... was not a personality contest."

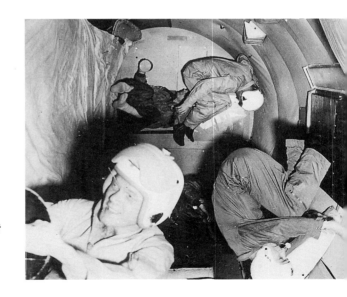

The astronauts learn coordination and balance in the weightless environment of a C-131 transport plane. Glenn is in the forefront.

Glenn knew that he was as qualified as anybody in the group to make the first flight. He had excelled during the training and the simulations and had mastered the Mercury flight plan and the capsule controls. Yet he also knew he might have trouble with a peer vote. Some of the others resented his leadership of the group, his clean-cut image, and his constant determination to outshine them in flight training, medical tests, and physical workouts. Glenn was an excellent pilot, but he was also an ambitious climber who knew how to ingratiate himself with his superiors to get what he wanted.

Glenn's worries about the peer vote were justified. The vote, held just before Christmas, went to Alan Shepard. On January 19, 1961, NASA announced the lineup for the first Mercury flight to the astronauts. Alan Shepard would ride the capsule; John Glenn and Gus Grissom would serve as his backups.

John Glenn standing beside a Mercury capsule during training

Chapter **FIVE**

THE FLIGHT OF *FRIENDSHIP* 7

THE PEER VOTE AND THE SELECTION OF ALAN Shepard as the first man in space disappointed and angered Glenn. Although Gilruth had not revealed the result of the vote to the astronauts, Glenn believed it had been the deciding factor in the selection. He felt sure he had been cheated out of his mission through a pointless popularity contest.

At Cape Canaveral, he went ahead with his preflight assignments and prepared to make the flight himself should anything happen to Shepard and Grissom. He knew he had to present a smiling face to the public because the selection had been kept secret. In the media, he was still considered the front-runner. At home, however, he withdrew into an angry silence that left his friends and family bewildered and frustrated.

Meanwhile, the United States seemed to be falling even further behind in the space race. On April 12, 1961, a twenty-seven-year-old Soviet cosmonaut (the Russian term for astronaut), Lieutenant Yuri Gagarin, had lifted off in the capsule *Vostok 1*. The rocket was launched from the Baikonur Cosmodrome in Kazakhstan, a republic in the hot, desertlike southern region of the Soviet Union. *Vostok 1* made a complete orbit of the Earth. After reentry, Gagarin ejected from the capsule near the town of Saratov. He was the first human to orbit the Earth.

Shepard's flight, officially Mercury 3, was scheduled for May 2. Early that morning, he climbed into his pressure suit, only to have the liftoff canceled due to bad weather. On the morning of May 5, 1961, workers moved the Redstone rocket and the Mercury capsule that Shepard had named *Freedom 7* to the launchpad

Gus Grissom prepares to enter the Liberty Bell 7 *spacecraft before rocketing 118 miles into space.*

Grissom hangs under the landing gear of the rescue helicopter that pulled him from the ocean.

at Cape Canaveral. Shepard climbed aboard but had to wait inside the capsule for four hours because a technical problem delayed the launch.

At 9:49 A.M. the *Freedom 7* was launched. After the Redstone booster separated, the capsule made a high arc, reaching 116.5 miles at apogee (the highest point of its orbit). Fifteen minutes after the launch, Shepard splashed down in the Atlantic Ocean, three hundred miles from the launchpad. The United States had completed its first successful crewed space mission.

On July 21, Gus Grissom made the second crewed Mercury flight in a capsule he called the *Liberty Bell 7*. Although the flight went well, Grissom had trouble after splashdown. For a reason neither Grissom nor flight engineers could explain, the explosive bolts of the hatch went off accidentally. Water rushed into the capsule, which began to sink. With his suit still on, Grissom managed to scramble out of the capsule, but soon felt himself being dragged down by the weight of the water that was leaking through an opening in his suit. A helicopter overhead managed to pull Grissom out of the water before he drowned, but the *Liberty Bell 7* sank to the bottom of the Atlantic Ocean.

After Grissom's flight, NASA and John Glenn began preparing for another suborbital mission. But on August 6, the Soviet Union took another important step ahead of the United States with the flight of cosmonaut Gherman Titov. In *Vostok 2*, Titov orbited the Earth sixteen times, spending more than an entire day in space.

Pressure from the public and the U.S. Congress, which controlled NASA's budget, grew stronger. NASA planners decided to stop the suborbital flights and proceed with an orbital flight using the Atlas booster rocket. John Glenn would be aboard. The Atlas rocket went through more tests in the fall of 1961. One test flight on November 28, 1961, carried a chimpanzee named Enos. The flight went off without a hitch.

Glenn's flight, officially named Mercury-Atlas 6, was scheduled for December 1961, but problems fitting the Mercury capsule atop the much larger Atlas booster delayed the launch. On January 16, 1962, problems with the propellant tanks caused another delay, and bad weather stopped the mission on January 23. Four days later, Glenn spent five hours suited up and ready inside the capsule, but heavy clouds over Cape Canaveral did not clear. The mission was postponed a total of ten times.

On February 20, 1962, Glenn again prepared for launch. This time, the weather held clear. At 9:47 A.M., the ninety-five-foot Atlas rocket ignited and the *Friendship 7* took off from Cape Canaveral. The Atlas lifted and turned toward the east, and the capsule began to shake and lurch as it approached the speed of sound. The acceleration built up to a force of 6 g's (six times the normal force of gravity on Earth). Glenn was pressed back into his seat as the force on his body increased his weight to about a thousand pounds. Monitors in his suit showed his pulse and blood pressure holding steady, however. Glenn had experienced high g forces many times before in the spaceflight simulators. After reaching a velocity of 17,500 miles an hour, the capsule separated from the booster rocket. At an altitude of about 550,000 feet, *Friendship 7* was flying fast enough and high enough to continue orbiting the Earth until slowed down by its own retro-rockets.

As the capsule reached orbital velocity, the g forces decreased until Glenn was weightless—free of the force of gravity. "Zero g and I feel fine," he exclaimed to ground controllers. "Oh, that view is tremendous!" Small thrusters on the capsule pitched it around 180 degrees and down 34 degrees to give Glenn a view of the Earth, one hundred miles beneath him. Flying backward, he could see immense dust storms in the Sahara Desert and an enormous ring of lights in Perth, Australia. The people of Perth had turned on every electric light in the city to greet the astronaut.

To his "capcom," or capsule communicator, Glenn described the first orbital sunset seen by a U.S. astronaut: "The speed at which the sun goes down is remarkable. The white line of the horizon, sandwiched between the black sky and dark Earth, is extremely bright as the sun sets. As the sun goes down a little bit more, the bottom layer becomes orange, and it fades into red and finally off into blues and black as you look farther up into space."

Glenn settled into the normal spaceflight routine of checklists and gauge readings while *Friendship 7*

John Glenn is inserted into the spacecraft Friendship 7 *during the last part of the countdown.*

crossed over the Pacific Ocean and again approached North America. If everything went smoothly, ground engineers had planned on *Friendship 7* making seven full orbits of the Earth, each of which would take about one and a half hours.

The capsule was not functioning smoothly, however. One of the small thrusters that controlled the attitude (orientation) of the capsule was not working, and Glenn felt the capsule begin to swing back and forth as the other thrusters fired to compensate. Glenn switched to manual control, overriding the automatic attitude control. He knew that if the problem wasn't corrected he would have to align the capsule for reentry himself. He would also have to preserve thruster fuel until the end of the flight. Without fuel, the cap-

Friendship 7 *takes off from Cape Canaveral, Florida, to orbit the Earth.*

sule would fly out of control.

Flight engineers on the ground encountered another problem during Glenn's first orbit. An indicator light reported that the protective landing bag on the end of the capsule had somehow deployed, but the ground controllers couldn't be sure. The indicator might have been malfunctioning, or the bag might actually have deployed. Positioned underneath the heat shield, the bag was not supposed to be used until after reentry. If it had deployed, the heat shield on *Friendship 7* might come loose. Without protection from the intense heat of reentry, Glenn and the capsule would burn up before splashdown.

The ground controllers decided to keep the information to themselves until Glenn's third orbit. Twice, without explaining why, they asked Glenn if the landing bag switch was in the "off" position inside the capsule, and twice he reported that it was. Finally, they had Glenn put the switch in the "automatic" position. A light inside the *Friendship 7* would then indicate whether the landing bag had, in fact, been deployed.

Surprised and angry that he had not been informed about their concern, Glenn hesitated. If the landing bag was still in its proper position, throwing the switch might deploy it accidentally. He moved his gloved hand slowly toward the control and then flipped the switch, staring at the indicator. "Negative," Glenn reported. "In automatic position, did not get a light, and I'm back in off position now. Over."

The time was approaching for reentry into the atmosphere. Using the retro-rockets on the back of the capsule, Glenn would have to maneuver *Friendship 7* to the correct angle. If the angle was too shallow, the capsule would skip off the atmosphere and back into space. If it was too steep, friction would burn it up. To make sure the heat shield stayed in place, flight engineers asked Glenn to fire the retro-rockets but then keep the retropack in place rather than jettisoning, or

Flight engineers watch as Friendship 7 *passes over Australia.*

discarding, it. The straps holding the rockets to the back of the capsule might help to secure the heat shield.

While orbiting above California, Glenn obeyed the orders from the ground, carefully checking the angle of the capsule and then firing the retro-rockets to begin slowing the spacecraft. The intense friction caused by the capsule gliding through the upper atmosphere of the Earth at tremendous speeds caused a cloud of flames and gas to surround *Friendship 7*. The intense heat caused radio interference that cut Glenn off from contact with the ground engineers. Outside his window, Glenn could see chunks of blazing metal flying away from the capsule. Were these fragments of

This photo was taken with an automatic camera inside the capsule as Glenn was orbiting the Earth.

the disintegrating heat shield or were they the retro-rockets? The capsule began to grow uncomfortably hot, but much to his relief, Glenn soon figured out that he was watching pieces of the retro-rocket apparatus burn up and fall away. Two parachutes deployed above the capsule, while a green light inside the capsule showed Glenn that the landing bag was deploying just as it was supposed to. At 2:43 P.M., after three orbits and four hours and fifty-six minutes of spaceflight, Glenn splashed down in the Atlantic Ocean eight hundred miles southeast of Cape Canaveral. The flight of *Friendship 7* was over.

Friendship 7 is being brought aboard the recovery ship after Glenn's successful orbital flight.

Chapter **SIX**

A FLIGHT INTO POLITICS

A FLEET OF DESTROYERS AND AIRCRAFT CARRI-
ers circled the landing zone, in the vicinity of Grand
Turk Island, searching for *Friendship 7*. Glenn remained inside the capsule, bobbing in the waves. Heat
built up inside the capsule and inside his pressure suit.
After twenty-one minutes, a helicopter picked up the
capsule and deposited it safely on the deck of the de-
stroyer *Noa*.

For Glenn and NASA, the flight had been merely
satisfactory. Glenn had completed three full orbits, but
he had experienced problems with the attitude controls on *Friendship 7* and a malfunctioning warning
light at ground control. Liftoff, orbital navigation,
communication, and reentry had gone well. The

capsule had been retrieved in one piece, and the astronaut had survived. Yet the astronauts and NASA scientists all knew that, in crewed as well as uncrewed spaceflight, the United States was still trying to catch up with the Soviet Union.

For the press and the public, however, Glenn's flight had been a heroic triumph. Finally, the United States seemed to be close to the Soviets in scientific achievement and in the Cold War battle for dominance in space. Glenn emerged as a winner at a time when the nation had suffered a long and discouraging string of defeats, not only in space but also in military and political battles on the ground. In the dawning age of powerful television images, Glenn's hardworking, clean-cut, all-American appearance further enhanced his appeal. "The attention lavished on him by the nation . . . could not be explained solely by the glamour of his flight," wrote journalist Frank Van Riper. "There seemed to be a quality about Glenn that attracted the public; an appearance, background and attitude which conjured up a view of the country that was equal parts fantasy and nostalgia."

John Kennedy had sensed these qualities when he had met and talked with Glenn before the flight. Having served in World War II as a naval officer, Kennedy greatly admired men who had courage and a sense of duty. He saw in Glenn much more than an astronaut. Kennedy believed Glenn might prove to be a valuable political ally in the upcoming election of 1964.

President John Kennedy presented Glenn with the NASA Distinguished Service Award. Next to Glenn are his wife, Annie, his daughter, Lyn, and his son David.

Kennedy flew to Cape Canaveral immediately after the flight of *Friendship 7* to congratulate Glenn during an elaborate ceremony. He then flew Glenn and his family back to Washington, D.C., aboard *Air Force One*, the official presidential jet. The president hosted a reception for Glenn at the White House and a parade down Pennsylvania Avenue. At the Capitol, Glenn gave a nationally televised speech to a joint session of Congress. On March 1, 1962 Glenn and the other Mercury astronauts rode in the largest ticker-tape parade in the history of New York City.

Glenn's success and sudden fame proved to be a great boost to the Mercury program. While planning several more orbital Mercury flights, NASA began working on President Kennedy's challenge to send a crewed space mission to the moon before the end of the decade. The Gemini program would be the next step in the process. Two-person capsules would remain in orbit for several days instead of hours, and astronauts would carry out docking and space-walking missions.

Glenn eagerly awaited the selection of the astronauts

who would take part in the Gemini program. Although he was over forty, Glenn believed his experience and ability merited another flight. To avoid any further risks to Glenn, however, President Kennedy passed the word to NASA that he wanted the astronaut permanently grounded. John Glenn didn't yet know it, but he had flown his last space mission for many years.

After the flight of *Friendship 7*, Glenn and his family moved to Houston, Texas, where NASA had recently established the new Manned Spaceflight Center. As a ground controller, Glenn took part in the Mercury flights of Scott Carpenter, Wally Schirra, and Gordon Cooper. (A heart condition prevented Deke Slayton from flying a Mercury mission.) But even while Glenn participated in the later Mercury flights, he had new careers and challenges on his mind.

Since high school, Glenn had excelled in public speaking. While rising through the ranks of the Marine Corps, his ambitious sense of duty to his country had also led him to thoughts of running for public office. He was one of the best-known and most admired individuals in the country, and he enjoyed President Kennedy's personal friendship and support. Glenn decided to run for the United States Senate.

Ohio senator Steve Young was running for reelection in the fall of 1964—the same year in which John Kennedy would be facing reelection. Knowing that a Glenn victory could help him, Kennedy passed the word to Steve Young that a high government post, possibly an ambassadorship, would be waiting for him if he withdrew from the race.

Young seriously considered the offer. He was a Democrat like Kennedy and Glenn, but he was seventy-four years old and already considering retirement from politics. Still, he enjoyed the Senate and had the strong support of the Ohio Democratic Party. The Democratic delegates already pledged to him seemed to assure his victory in the Ohio primary, scheduled for May 1964. During the primary election, the Ohio Democrats and Republicans would select their final candidates for the general election in the fall.

Then, on November 22, 1963, President Kennedy was assassinated while riding in a motorcade in Dallas, Texas. Vice President Lyndon Johnson became the new president, and the deal with Steve Young was off. Robert Kennedy, one of John Kennedy's brothers, advised his friend John Glenn that it might be best to stand aside for this election.

Although Glenn had no organization backing him and almost no money, he decided to run for the Senate anyway. On January 17, three days before the Ohio Democratic convention, he announced his candidacy. It had been almost two years since his Mercury flight, but Glenn believed those five hours in space would be enough to bring him a stunning, come-from-behind political victory.

Glenn's 1964 campaign got off to a slow start. By

a law known as the Hatch Act, federal employees, including members of the military, are barred from any partisan political activity. Although Glenn had officially retired from the space program in January 1964, he was still a marine. Making political speeches, appearing in political ads, and passing out campaign literature were activities that were still against the law for Glenn—and he would not break or even bend the law. During the convention in Columbus, he remained in his hotel suite, simply greeting well-wishers who came up to his room from the convention floor to meet him and get his autograph.

Nevertheless, Glenn's informal conversations with the delegates were enough to bring a slight majority of them over to his side. Fearing his rising popularity, a group of Young supporters offered Glenn an open seat in the House of Representatives if he would give up his challenge to Steve Young. Glenn refused. He wanted a seat in the Senate. Many of the delegates began to worry that the elderly Young might lose to a Republican in November. They thought Glenn, the heroic outsider who was nearly half Young's age, might have a better chance of winning. After taking a floor vote, the convention pronounced itself deadlocked, unable to endorse either Young or Glenn.

Although the campaign began without endorsement for either candidate, Glenn still thought he could win. He filed for his resignation from the Marine Corps. While waiting for the orders to come through,

Glenn traveled throughout the state of Ohio, attracting large crowds of enthusiastic well-wishers. Because the Hatch Act still prevented him from taking a political stand, he expressed few opinions on the issues. He believed that his heroism would be enough to gain him a victory. Actually, for many important issues, he still hadn't formed an opinion. He had had little time as an astronaut to think about civil rights, worsening crime and poverty in large cities, the problems in the public schools, or the country's involvement in the Vietnam War. Glenn simply invited the public to give him *their* opinion—which proved to be a refreshing change for many voters.

By late February, the campaign was in full swing. Then an accident abruptly stopped John Glenn's political career. On February 26, he suffered a fall in the bathroom at his apartment in Columbus, Ohio. His head struck the side of the bathtub, causing a concussion and a buildup of fluid in his inner ear. Suffering nausea, dizziness, and great difficulty walking, Glenn spent several weeks in the hospital. In the meantime, Annie Glenn and Rene Carpenter, the wife of Scott Carpenter, campaigned in John's place. By March 30, Glenn still wasn't feeling well, so he dropped out of the race.

Steve Young went on to win the primary by a 5-to-2 margin. That fall, Lyndon Johnson won the presidential election, and Young edged out his Republican challenger, Robert Taft.

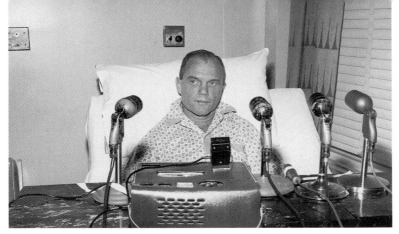

From his hospital bed at Lackland Air Force Base, Glenn told the media he was withdrawing from the campaign. He had been hospitalized after a fall.

Glenn returned to his home near Houston to rest and slowly recover from his head injury. For several months, he could barely walk around his house, but gradually his health and his balance improved. In the meantime, he was facing another difficult situation. Retired from NASA and drawing only a military salary, he would have to find a new way to support his family. Debts from the Ohio primary campaign still haunted him—he owed sixteen thousand dollars. Instead of holding a political fund-raiser to meet the debt, he decided to pay it off himself. That decision almost wiped out the family's savings.

John Glenn was still a widely recognized name, however, and he was receiving offers from corporations to endorse products or join company boards of directors. In October 1964, Glenn accepted an offer from the Royal Crown Cola company to work as a vice president and serve on the board of directors. Within a short time, he was named president of Royal Crown International, the department that promoted and sold

Royal Crown Cola outside the United States. As his children entered college, Glenn moved into a comfortable apartment furnished by his employer in New York City.

Glenn also used contacts he had made in Florida to enter the hotel business. He went into partnership with an old friend of his named Henri Landwirth, who owned several properties in Cocoa Beach. The two men formed a company to develop more hotels in Florida, a state that was booming with retirees and younger people seeking a warm climate. Glenn and Landwirth bid for a Holiday Inn franchise, the right to build and operate a hotel using the Holiday Inn name. One of these valuable franchises was in the city of Orlando, near the new Disney World theme park.

Glenn and Landwirth were awarded the Orlando franchise and several others. With the popularity of Disney World and other attractions near Orlando, the hotel venture proved to be a huge success, bringing Glenn an income of several hundred thousand dollars a year. In the meantime, Glenn had accepted seats on the boards of several other corporations, jobs which required only that he take part in board meetings and make informed decisions about company policies. In the mid-1960s, John Glenn grew wealthy within the space of just a few years—but he never forgot his ambition to serve in the United States Senate.

An aide holds Senator Robert Kennedy as he stands on a seat while campaigning for the 1968 Democratic presidential nomination in California.

Chapter **SEVEN**

1968

JOHN **G**LENN **WAS** **NEVER** **SATISFIED** **WITH** **COM-** fort, wealth, and national fame. He continually sought new challenges. In 1968, while searching for another chance to enter the political arena, he seized an opportunity to join the presidential campaign of Robert Kennedy.

Robert Kennedy and John Glenn had remained close friends after the assassination of President John Kennedy. While Kennedy greatly admired Glenn's courage and character, Glenn learned much from Kennedy's grasp of political and social issues. Kennedy was a strong supporter of civil and voting rights for minorities. He spoke out on behalf of the country's urban poor, and he was also popular on college campuses as a critic of the Vietnam War. Glenn soon learned that Kennedy was a tireless politician. From Kennedy, Glenn learned how to organize a national campaign, raise money, and use the media. Glenn also realized that a Kennedy victory might well bring him appointment to a high federal office.

Early in 1968, states began holding primary elections to choose the candidates that would contend for the presidential nomination at the Democratic National Convention. The candidate who won the nomination would then run for president against the Republican nominee in the November general election. Public opinion polls showed that President Lyndon Johnson and his challenger, Senator Eugene McCarthy of Minnesota, were running in close com-

Senator Eugene McCarthy gives a "V" for victory sign after winning the 1968 Democratic presidential primary election in Wisconsin.

President Lyndon Johnson tells the nation that he will not run for reelection in 1968.

petition. Opposition to the Vietnam War and serious racial unrest in the United States caused many people to question President Johnson's ability to continue to lead the nation. In the March 12 New Hampshire primary, Johnson barely defeated McCarthy in the popular vote, while McCarthy managed to capture most of the state's delegates to the Democratic National Convention. Soon afterward, Robert Kennedy announced that he, too, would oppose Johnson and run for the Democratic presidential nomination. On March 31, Lyndon Johnson shocked the nation by announcing that he was withdrawing from the race and would not run for reelection.

Johnson's vice president, Hubert Humphrey of Minnesota, then entered the race, making the 1968 Democratic nomination a three-way contest. Glenn accepted Robert Kennedy's invitation to join his campaign. Worried that his image was too liberal for many voters, Kennedy believed that Glenn's military record and heroic image would help him win the support of conservative Democrats. Although Glenn supported

Kennedy's stance on domestic issues, he differed on Vietnam. Kennedy wanted an immediate withdrawal of U.S. troops; Glenn believed that the government should officially declare war and give the military better means to finish and win it.

By the time of the California primary on June 5, Kennedy and McCarthy were running neck and neck. California was probably the single most important state in the entire campaign, having more electoral votes than any state except New York. Kennedy won the primary by a narrow margin of 4.5 percent—just enough to keep him ahead of McCarthy until the convention.

That night, after Kennedy's victory was officially declared on television, he left his fifth-floor suite and went down to the ballroom of the Ambassador Hotel in Los Angeles to give a rousing speech to a crowd of

John Glenn, right, *attends a fund-raiser with Senator Robert Kennedy and his wife, Ethel.*

Vice President Hubert Humphrey won the Democratic presidential nomination in 1968.

cheering supporters. Glenn remained upstairs. After finishing the speech, Kennedy left the podium and walked back to the hotel kitchen to avoid the crowd. Suddenly, a short, thin, young man named Sirhan Sirhan emerged, aimed a pistol at Kennedy's head, and began firing. The senator fell to the floor, bleeding from a deep bullet wound.

Within seconds of hearing the news, Glenn rushed down to the kitchen. Kennedy was lifted from the floor, placed into an ambulance, and rushed to a hospital for emergency surgery. His wife, Ethel Kennedy, asked Glenn to break the news to the six Kennedy children, who had accompanied their father to California. Glenn did so, and on the following day accompanied the children back to their home in Virginia, while Ethel remained in California with her husband. On the following night, Robert Kennedy died. Glenn then took on the difficult job of telling the Kennedy children that their father had passed away.

John Glenn had lost a close friend and an important political ally. Glenn's political career had again come to an abrupt halt.

The Ohio National Guard converge on Kent State University as students protest U.S. involvement in the Vietnam War.

Chapter **EIGHT**

BATTLES IN OHIO

IN 1970, STEVE YOUNG ANNOUNCED THAT HE would retire from the United States Senate. John Glenn again saw his chance—a better chance, he thought, than he had had in 1964. To the public, he was still the hero of *Friendship 7*. He could point to success in business and to a close friendship with Robert Kennedy, one of the most popular Democratic politicians of the 1960s.

Glenn again announced his candidacy for the Senate, but so did Howard Metzenbaum, a Cleveland businessman, former state legislator, and Steve Young's campaign manager. Metzenbaum was not as well known as Glenn, and he was Jewish—in a state that had never nominated or elected a Jewish candidate to

John Glenn, left, *and Howard Metzenbaum* right, *both seek victory in the 1970 Ohio Democratic primary election. The man in the center is unidentified.*

a major office. But Metzenbaum did have political experience and the support of Ohio's strong labor unions. He also had plenty of money. He hired professional campaign advisers and appeared in television spots that made the voters familiar with his name and his liberal message.

But Glenn felt confident that with his name known to almost every voter in the country, he could beat Metzenbaum in the Ohio Democratic primary. He put together a small, inexperienced campaign staff and, instead of spending money on expensive television spots, decided to reserve it for the fall campaign against the Republican nominee. Glenn didn't worry about developing ties with the Ohio Democratic Party, most of whose members still saw him as too conservative. He still believed his fame as an astronaut and his association with the Kennedys would attract enough votes to win the primary.

Glenn soon realized that he had underestimated Howard Metzenbaum, however. Metzenbaum's experience as a labor lawyer earned him high ranks among Ohio's strong industrial unions. His liberal stand on issues such as welfare, civil rights, and public spending gained him support in urban areas such as Cleveland and Toledo. Metzenbaum hired a big staff to distribute campaign literature and make fund-raising and get-out-the-vote phone calls. By running an effective campaign and outspending Glenn, he made his name and image familiar to Ohio voters.

In his campaign speeches, Metzenbaum also made a point of directly criticizing President Richard Nixon's handling of the Vietnam War. Glenn, whose military training had instilled in him a great respect for the office of commander in chief, would not criticize Nixon's actions, despite the fact that he disagreed with him. On May 4, 1970—the day before the Ohio Democratic primary—Vietnam and the antiwar movement

The Ohio National Guard open fire on Kent State protestors, killing four students.

became even more important in the voters' minds. On that day, four students at Kent State University in Ohio were shot and killed by members of the Ohio National Guard during an antiwar protest. The shootings shocked voters and nudged many of them to support Metzenbaum. On May 5, Glenn won almost all of Ohio's rural counties, while Metzenbaum won the much larger blocs of votes in Ohio's big cities, as well as the primary itself.

Once again, an opportunity for the Senate had slipped by John Glenn. This time, there had been no accident. Glenn's poor campaign strategy and lack of organization had allowed Metzenbaum to achieve a come-from-behind primary victory. Glenn reluctantly endorsed Metzenbaum for the fall election and then joined the campaign of John Gilligan, who was running for Ohio governor. Glenn made speeches on Gilligan's behalf and appeared in several television spots. That November, Gilligan won the governor's race, while Howard Metzenbaum lost to Republican Robert Taft Jr. in the Senate race.

Many people believed John Glenn's political career had ended. But Glenn was looking forward to the 1974 election, when Republican senator William Saxbe would be running for reelection. By this time Glenn had learned that to win high office, he had to participate wholeheartedly in Ohio politics. He moved to Columbus, the state capital, and made Ohio his permanent residence. He also took a more active part

John Glenn, left, *chair of the Ohio Citizen's Task Force on Environmental Protection, presents a copy of the task force report to Governor John Gilligan,* right.

in the state Democratic organization. Governor Gilligan awarded Glenn for his campaign work by appointing him to an environmental task force, which helped to write a new law establishing a state environmental agency. Glenn traveled around the state, making speeches, meeting the public, doing favors, and collecting the support and goodwill necessary for his next campaign.

Meanwhile, the national political scene was in turmoil. A scandal had broken out over a burglary at Democratic National Committee headquarters in Washington, D.C., during the 1972 presidential campaign. Richard Nixon had won reelection that year, but the president and several of his key aides had tried to cover up the burglary and illegally block the investigation that was underway. Public pressure

*Harvard Law School
professor Archibald Cox*

forced Nixon to appoint a special prosecutor, Harvard
Law School professor Archibald Cox, to conduct an
official inquiry. In the fall of 1973, Cox learned of secret tape recordings Nixon had made in the White
House and demanded that the president turn them
over to a Senate investigating committee. When Nixon
refused, Cox filed petitions in court to obtain the
tapes. On Saturday night, October 20, 1973, Nixon ordered Attorney General Elliot Richardson to fire Cox,
but Richardson refused to do so and resigned. Nixon
ordered Deputy Attorney General William D. Ruckelshaus to dismiss Cox, but Ruckelshaus resigned as
well. Finally, Nixon asked Solicitor General Robert H.
Bork to fire Cox, and Bork agreed to do so. The
events of that night became known as the Saturday
Night Massacre.

Attorney General William Saxbe, left, *with President Richard Nixon,* right

Nixon appointed William Saxbe to replace Richardson as attorney general. As a result, Saxbe had to resign his Ohio Senate seat, and Governor Gilligan had to appoint someone to replace the senator. Both John Glenn and Howard Metzenbaum sought the appointment, but Gilligan wanted Glenn to be his running mate in the 1974 election. Gilligan also thought that by appointing Metzenbaum to the vacant Senate seat, he could gain the support of organized labor—support he would need for the 1974 campaign.

Glenn was not interested in being Gilligan's lieutenant governor, however. Glenn announced that he would run for the Senate in 1974 with or without the endorsement of Gilligan and the state Democratic party leaders. Gilligan appointed Metzenbaum to fill William Saxbe's Senate seat. Within months, John Glenn and Howard Metzenbaum were battling again for the Ohio Democratic nomination for the Senate.

John Glenn flashes a big smile after learning that he would be the Democratic nominee for the U.S. Senate in Ohio.

Chapter **NINE**

ROOKIE IN THE SENATE

FOR SEVERAL MONTHS IN LATE **1973** AND EARLY 1974, Howard Metzenbaum and John Glenn confronted each other in a rough and bitter political campaign. This time, John Glenn was the underdog. His opponent had the support of the state's Democratic Party and most Democratic voters.

Glenn still had no experience as an elected legislator. He relied on his exploits as a war hero and an astronaut and criticized Metzenbaum's much safer career as a wealthy lawyer and businessman. (The military had rejected Metzenbaum for active service during World War II because of his poor eyesight.) Metzenbaum stressed his public service as a state legislator. He had been the youngest member of the Ohio

House of Representatives in history and had supported antidiscrimination and prolabor laws in the 1940s and 1950s, when such measures were still unpopular with many Ohio voters.

Glenn toured the state's counties in a luxurious bus. He stopped at shopping malls, senior citizens' homes, factories—anywhere he could find a gathering of people. At each stop, he shook hands and made "stump" speeches—named after an old tradition of giving short speeches from tree stumps. Yet early polls showed that Glenn's campaign was failing to make any progress against Metzenbaum. In February 1974, Glenn decided to hire Steve Kovacik, an experienced, professional manager, to run his campaign. Kovacik changed the focus from county seats and small towns, which he believed Glenn would probably win anyway. Kovacik scheduled appearances in Ohio's cities in an effort to capture some of Metzenbaum's supporters among union members and ethnic minorities.

Following Kovacik's advice, Glenn made an issue of Metzenbaum's wealth and his ability to avoid paying taxes by using tax shelters—legal methods of keeping the money he earned from being taxed. Glenn released his own tax returns, which showed that he had paid much more federal tax than Metzenbaum, even though he had earned much less. This action embarrassed Metzenbaum, who suddenly looked more clever than honest. Glenn pressed his advantage by demanding that Metzenbaum make a full public disclosure of his tax returns as well as his personal assets and debts. Glenn tried to connect Metzenbaum's financial entanglements to questions of morality raised by the Watergate scandal.

Metzenbaum responded by accusing Glenn of being a closet Republican—a man whose real views on the issues were at odds with the majority of Democratic voters. He also remarked that Glenn had "never held a job," a dig at Glenn's long service as a member of the U.S. military and his years on the government payroll as a NASA astronaut.

Glenn knew that Metzenbaum's remark gave him a good opportunity to retaliate. At a debate on May 3, just before the primary vote, Glenn made a short, stinging speech rebuking Metzenbaum for his comment and recounting the deeds of brave soldiers and veterans who had risked their lives fighting in foreign countries. The speech made headlines across the state and clinched Glenn's primary victory by ninety-one thousand votes. That November, Glenn easily defeated his Republican challenger, Ralph Perk of Cleveland, by carrying every county in Ohio. Finally, the astronaut had become a senator.

John Glenn joined ninety-nine other senators in the Ninety-fourth Congress, which began in January 1975. Glenn spent long hours in his Senate office, studying books and papers on current issues, such as education, taxes, the military, and foreign affairs. Like every new senator, Glenn lobbied senior members of his party for committee assignments that interested him. Eventually these senior members appointed him to the Armed Services Committee, the Governmental Affairs Committee, and the Senate Select Intelligence Committee. Each of these committees debated and voted on new laws proposed by other members of the Senate. Gradually, as Glenn spent more years in the Senate, he built up seniority of his own. In 1986, as the senior member of the Governmental Affairs Committee, he became its chairperson.

Although he was one of the most famous members of the Senate, Glenn did not always get along with his colleagues. He did not like to compromise his views or make deals with his political opponents to get new laws passed. Glenn also had trouble raising money for his friends and for himself. He didn't like fund-raising events, where politicians meet hundreds of people for a brief time in an effort to raise money.

During Glenn's first few months in the Senate, the national political landscape began to change in favor of the Democrats. On the morning of August 9, 1974, Nixon resigned as president. At noon that day, Vice President Gerald Ford took the oath of office and replaced Nixon as president of the United States. Ford's administration suffered from declining public confidence in government, inflation (rising prices), and increasing unemployment.

Meanwhile, political candidates were seeking an image as "outsiders" who had stayed as far as possible from "politics as usual" in Washington, D.C. Governor Jimmy Carter of Georgia—a man with no experience whatsoever in Washington—became the front-runner for the 1976 presidential nomination at the Democratic National Convention.

Party leaders chose John Glenn, who was still considered more astronaut than politician, as one of the convention's keynote speakers, an important role. Many people believed Glenn might even convince Jimmy Carter to choose him as a vice presidential running mate.

On July 12, Glenn appeared on national television to personally endorse the Democratic Party and its programs. He mounted the podium in New York's Madison Square Garden to deliver the most important speech of his career. In an earnest and serious tone, Glenn gave a long talk about making government more responsive to the voters. The speech was dry and flat. Within minutes, everyone in the hall—and

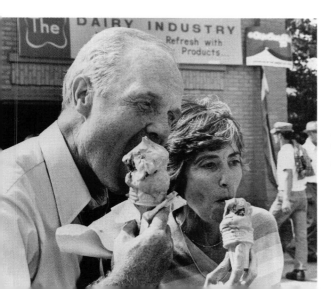

Senator Glenn and his wife, Annie, enjoy ice cream cones at the 1976 Ohio state fair.

Senator John Glenn addresses the 1976 Democratic National Convention.

most people in the television audience—were paying attention to something else. Glenn offered no rousing phrases in support of the Democrats and no stinging attacks on the Republicans. Many of the bored delegates inside Madison Square Garden simply got up and left their chairs to walk around, chat with friends, or buy a snack. After finishing the speech, Glenn left the podium to polite but sparse applause.

After watching Glenn's speech in his hotel room, Jimmy Carter went over a short list of names he had drawn up as possible vice presidential running mates. He had already decided to choose a member of Congress, because he himself had no experience as a Washington legislator. The week before the convention, he had invited several senators to his home in Plains, Georgia, including Glenn, Walter Mondale from Minnesota, and Edmund Muskie from Maine. During the meeting, Mondale and Carter had struck up a close friendship. Carter was already leaning toward Mondale, and John Glenn's long-winded speech at the New York convention confirmed his decision.

In November, Jimmy Carter won the presidential election. Glenn continued his work in the Senate, supporting Carter's programs for the most part, giving short speeches in the Senate chamber, attending committee meetings, and welcoming visitors from his home state. Although he was still a rookie, Glenn enjoyed success as a lawmaker, winning ten roll-call votes on his own amendments (changes to laws) during his first year. (Roll-call votes are held when "aye!" or "nay!" voice votes are too close to call.) The voters of Ohio were satisfied with the job Glenn was doing, and they reelected him to the Senate in 1980.

By the 1980s, NASA and the space program had undergone many important changes. In 1967, astronauts Gus Grissom, Roger Chaffee, and Ed White had died in a launchpad fire that ignited the *Apollo 1* capsule. But on July 20, 1969, during the flight of *Apollo 11*, astronauts Neil Armstrong and Buzz Aldrin became the first humans to walk on the moon.

After several more moon landings, the Apollo program came to an end, and the United States began work on *Skylab*—the first American space station. *Skylab's* first flight took place in 1973. Three separate crews went to the station to make observations and conduct experiments. After *Skylab*, NASA prepared an entirely new space vehicle, the space shuttle *Columbia*. The shuttle was designed to reach orbit and remain in space for several weeks, then return to Earth by landing on a runway—like a jet airplane. It could then be

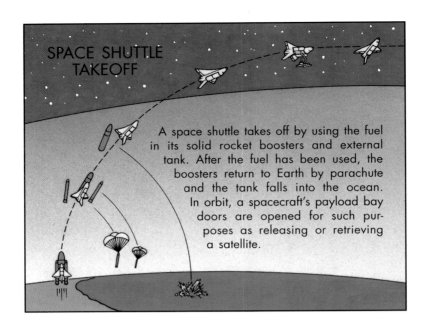

SPACE SHUTTLE TAKEOFF

A space shuttle takes off by using the fuel in its solid rocket boosters and external tank. After the fuel has been used, the boosters return to Earth by parachute and the tank falls into the ocean. In orbit, a spacecraft's payload bay doors are opened for such purposes as releasing or retrieving a satellite.

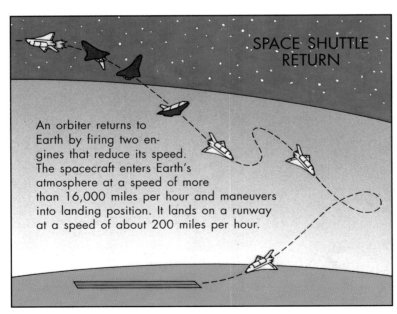

SPACE SHUTTLE RETURN

An orbiter returns to Earth by firing two engines that reduce its speed. The spacecraft enters Earth's atmosphere at a speed of more than 16,000 miles per hour and maneuvers into landing position. It lands on a runway at a speed of about 200 miles per hour.

returned to orbit by another launch. The first shuttle flight took place on April 12, 1981.

Another shuttle, the *Challenger,* made several missions to conduct experiments and repair damaged satellites. But on January 28, 1986, the *Challenger* exploded just after lifting off from Cape Canaveral. Seven astronauts died in the explosion, and the shuttle program was suspended.

Meanwhile, John Glenn remained in the Senate. In the Ohio Senate race of 1980, he won an easy victory with sixty-nine percent of the vote. Ohio voters were familiar with Glenn and liked his moderate political ideas, which were neither too conservative nor too liberal. In Washington, Glenn had also become a respected expert on nuclear arms control between the Soviet Union and the United States.

Glenn's years of service on the Governmental Affairs Committee also made him an expert on the complicated details of how the federal government operates from

Astronauts Neil Armstrong, left, *and Edwin (Buzz) Aldrin standing on the surface of the moon*

day to day. He could talk for hours about such details but still took little interest in tackling more emotional issues—such as income taxes and education—that voters cared about. In 1984, Glenn entered several primary elections for the Democratic presidential nomination. On the national election stage, he still suffered from his reputation as an honest, serious, but dull politician. After running behind in several important primaries, he dropped out of the race, and Walter Mondale eventually won the nomination.

Glenn in Massachusetts, running for the Democratic presidential nomination in 1984

Glenn won reelection to the Senate in 1986, with 62 percent of the Ohio vote. In the Senate, he continued to focus on military and government affairs. He helped to establish and gain cabinet status for the Department of Veterans Affairs. Glenn also sponsored a law that would make the Environmental Protection Agency a part of the president's cabinet. In this effort, however, he faced opposition from Republicans and from President George Bush.

In the late 1980s, scandal brushed Glenn's political career. It was discovered that several congressmen had done important favors for the operators of savings and loan associations. After many of these savings and loans went bankrupt in the mid-1980s, the Department of Justice began an investigation. In the spring and summer of 1987, federal investigators discovered that savings and loan directors had spent depositors' money on risky investments and enormous salaries for

Senator Glenn, third from the left, *testifying before the Senate Ethics Committee*

Senator Glenn announcing legislation to restructure the Federal Emergency Management Agency at a news conference. Senator Dianne Feinstein stands to the right.

themselves. Charles Keating, a savings and loan operator from California, was at the center of the scandal. Keating had once been a Cincinnati, Ohio, businessman. He had also been a close friend of Glenn's since Glenn's 1970 campaign, when the two men first met.

In 1988, while the investigation was underway, Glenn arranged a meeting between Keating and the Speaker of the House, Jim Wright of Texas. Wright could have done important favors for Keating—even interfered with the Justice Department investigation. Voters, colleagues, and investigators began to suspect Glenn of exchanging political favors for campaign contributions from Keating and other savings and loans operators. Although the investigation eventually cleared Glenn of this charge, the Senate Ethics Committee officially reported that Glenn had "exercised poor judgment."

In 1990, the Persian Gulf War broke out when Iraq invaded Kuwait. President George Bush prepared for an attack on Iraq to defeat the invasion, and in early

1991 the Senate passed the Gulf War Resolution supporting Bush's action. Glenn opposed the measure,
however, believing that the United States should not
take a direct part in the fight. After the United States
and its allies defeated Iraq, Glenn sponsored laws that
would allow financial help to Gulf War veterans and
their families. At a time when many men and women
who had taken part in the conflict were contracting
mysterious illnesses caused by chemical weapons used
in the war, Glenn sponsored a law to improve the
health benefits of Gulf War veterans.

In 1992, Glenn was reelected but with only 51 per-

*President Bill Clinton gestures as he shakes hands with Senator
Glenn after signing the Federal Acquisitions Streamlining Act
of 1994.*

cent of the vote. His main problem was the Keating savings and loan scandal, which had affected his popularity in Ohio. But with the election of Democrat Bill Clinton to the presidency that same year, a member of Glenn's own party moved into the White House for the first time in 12 years.

President Bill Clinton and Vice President Al Gore had promised to make the huge federal government more efficient—an issue that seriously concerned the voters who had elected them. Glenn helped to pass new laws that cut the federal workforce, cut federal spending, streamlined the system of government purchasing, and reduced government paperwork.

Glenn also continued his efforts to stop the proliferation (spread) of nuclear weapons. Since the 1980s, he had supported laws that banned the sale of nuclear material to India and Pakistan, two hostile neighbors in southern Asia that have access to nuclear weapons. Glenn made hundreds of public statements about nuclear arms issues and became a leading voice in the duel between the United States and Iraq over Iraq's efforts to build nuclear weapons.

In February 1997, Glenn announced that he would not run for a fifth Senate term in the fall of 1998. He was in his mid-seventies by this time, and his thoughts were turning away from Washington, D.C., toward a possible return to space.

On January 16, 1998, NASA announced that after 36 years, Senator John Glenn would be returning to

At Muskingum College, Glenn announces that he will not run for reelection in 1998.

space aboard the shuttle *Discovery.* Ever since his splashdown aboard *Friendship 7,* Glenn had been preparing for a return to space and had kept in contact with NASA leaders. In the 1980s and 1990s, Glenn had repeatedly suggested to NASA directors the idea of a return flight. Since his first training in New Philadelphia, Glenn had collected more than fifty-four hundred hours of flying time, including nearly two thousand in jets. Ability and experience would be no obstacle at a time when civilian scientists, teachers—even congressmen such as Senator Jake Garn of Utah and Representative Bill Nelson of Florida—were riding the shuttle.

By 1995, Glenn was taking a strong interest in the affairs of the elderly. He realized that as the number of elderly people increased, issues such as health affairs and health insurance, Social Security, and retirement pensions were becoming more important. Glenn had noticed that the physical effects of aging parallel many of the effects of weightlessness and spaceflight. He proposed to NASA that he return to space to study those effects firsthand.

During a long period of weightlessness aboard an orbiting spacecraft, many astronauts experience disrupted sleep, loss of bone mass, loss of coordination, and a weakening of the body's immune system. Is it a coincidence that many of these symptoms are also experienced by many elderly people? Or is there some parallel between the environment of spaceflight and Earthbound aging? Even young people experience a brief, temporary speeding up of the aging process in space. Glenn believed an elderly astronaut might be able to answer these questions, and that he was the right candidate for the job.

NASA considered Glenn's request for more than a year. Eventually, NASA director Daniel Goldin had to weigh the good publicity of returning John Glenn to space against the risks of Glenn's possible injury or death—an event that might have an even worse effect on the space program than the tragic deaths aboard *Apollo 1* or the shuttle *Challenger*. Finally, Goldin decided that he had enough confidence in the shuttle and in Glenn to take the risk. On January 16, 1998, NASA made the official announcement: John Glenn would be aboard *Discovery*.

The space shuttle Discovery lifts off its launchpad with John Glenn and six other astronauts aboard for a nine-day flight.

Chapter **TEN**

THE FLIGHT OF *DISCOVERY*

ON **OCTOBER 29, 1998,** *DISCOVERY* **LIFTED** from its launchpad at Cape Canaveral, Florida, and roared into orbit. On board were Chiaki Mukai, Pedro Duque, Scott Parazynski, Steven Lindsey, Curtis Brown Jr., flight commander Stephen Robinson, and Senator John Glenn. It had been thirty-six years and eight months since Glenn's last spaceflight aboard *Friendship 7*. This time instead of flying solo in a cramped capsule, he was part of a seven-member crew riding aboard a spacious orbiting laboratory. He would make 134 orbits rather than 3 and would cover a total distance of 3.6 million miles. If all went well, *Discovery* would remain aloft for nine days.

Glenn's assignment as payload specialist made him

Chiaki Mukai, left, *and John Glenn,* right, *on the mid-deck of one of the shuttle training mockups at the Johnson Space Center.*

responsible for conducting many of the eighty-nine experiments carried out aboard *Discovery* during its nine-day mission. Payload specialists are responsible for overseeing the various devices, including satellites, experimental apparatus, and measuring tools, that are brought into orbit in the shuttle's cargo hold.

But Glenn's primary mission was to conduct experiments on himself. Before, during, and after the flight, Glenn gave a total of thirty blood samples as part of a "protein turnover experiment." This test measured the buildup and breakdown of proteins in the blood. Glenn also gave sixteen urine samples. For sleep experiments, Glenn wore a special sleep-study suit. The suit measured his brain waves, eye movement, breathing, and chest expansion.

Glenn measured his body temperature, blood pressure,

and bone mass. He also took samples from the rest of the crew as an experimental control. After *Discovery* returned to Earth, these measurements were compared to measurements taken just before the flight, while Glenn was training on the ground. Changes in his physical state while in orbit were then compared to his "normal" state on the ground. Scientists sifted through the many pages of data for clues about the parallel effects of spaceflight and aging on the body. The results will help NASA make decisions about using elderly astronauts on future missions.

The flight of *Discovery* went well. Only one minor problem occurred on liftoff, when a cover panel for the compartment holding the shuttle's drogue parachute tumbled to the ground. The loss of the panel meant that *Discovery* could not use the chute, which

Payload specialist John Glenn, equipped with sleep-monitoring equipment, stands near his sleep station on the mid-deck of the space shuttle Discovery.

COMPARE AND CONTRAST

	Friendship 7	Discovery
Altitude (miles)	162	325
Circuit breakers	20	961
Computers aboard	0	5
Crew Space (cubic feet)	36	2,325
Distance (miles)	75,679	3,600,000
Flight time	4 hours, 56 minutes	144 hours
Items aboard	48	2,600
Launch site	Cape Canaveral Air Station Cape Canaveral, Florida	Kennedy Space Center Cape Canaveral, Florida
Maximum g's	7.7	3
Orbits	3	144
Passengers	1 (male)	7 (6 males, 1 female)
Push buttons	8	219
Toggle switches	56	856
Windows	1	10
Year of flight	1962	1998

Sources: Newsweek, Oct. 26,1998; Minneapolis Star Tribune, Oct. 18, 1998

Glenn works on an experiment inside the space-lab facility on board Discovery.

slows and stabilizes the craft as it lands. As in *Friendship 7,* Glenn faced a problem during the critical stage of reentry and landing.

In fact, many shuttle landings had occurred without parachutes—and without problems. *Discovery* did so, too. On November 7, the shuttle returned to Earth. With two sonic booms (caused by shock waves from a large craft moving faster than the speed of sound), *Discovery* reentered the atmosphere and touched down at Cape Canaveral about 1:00 P.M.

After leaving *Discovery,* John Glenn declared, "One g and I feel fine!" His second trip into space had been a success, but he was glad to return to Earth. He knew it would be his last flight—he had made a promise to Annie that from then on he would remain grounded.

Glenn's 134 orbits brought back public interest in a shuttle flight and generated good publicity for the

NASA space program. Most importantly, it symbolized the ability of an elderly person to take on difficult physical and mental challenges—an important lesson in a society that often underestimates the elderly.

But Glenn's *Discovery* mission drew controversy as well as admiration. Some writers described it as a publicity stunt or as a congressional "junket" (a free trip without serious goals). They pointed out that several other elderly candidates had also been available, and that choosing Glenn was only an attempt by NASA to curry favor with Congress.

Others reacted more favorably. To many people, John Glenn still remained a hero for facing the unknowns of orbital flight aboard *Friendship 7*. They saw Glenn's return to space at the age of seventy-seven as another act of courage, and his mission aboard *Discovery* as a reminder of what the nation can accomplish. "Never mind that the carpers call this mission useless," Roger Rosenblatt wrote in *Time* magazine. "The public does not require a usefulness beyond its own admiring pleasure. As for the practicalities of the space program, it was never so useful as when it reminded the country of heroic capabilities."

On Monday, November 16, 1998, John and Annie Glenn rode together in a parade through New York City. At a ceremony, Mayor Rudolph Giuliani made a welcoming speech and presented Glenn with the keys to the city. Once again, Glenn had replayed a scene from 1962, when he was given what was then the

Astronaut John Glenn waves to the cheering crowds as he and Annie ride in an open car during a ticker tape parade in New York City on November 16, 1998.

largest ticker-tape parade in New York's history.

The parade provided John Glenn with a spectacular finish to his long career as a military pilot, pioneering astronaut, and four-term Ohio senator. As the central figure in a noisy parade, Glenn was again playing the role that he had begun more than fifty years before in the skies over the Marshall Islands of the Pacific: American hero.

SOURCES

31　Frank Van Riper, Glenn: *The Astronaut Who Would Be President* (New York: Empire Books, 1983), 118.

33　Tom Wolfe, *The Right Stuff* (New York: Farrar, Straus and Girous, 1979), 60.

38　Donald K. Slayton with Michael Cassutt, *Deke! U.S. Manned Space: From Mercury to the Shuttle* (New York: Tom Doherty Associates Inc., 1994), 73.

39　Ibid., 74.

44　Wolfe, 180.

54　Peter Bond, *Heroes in Space: From Gagarin to Challenger* (New York: Basil Blackwell, 1987), 41.

56　Wolfe, 281.

60　Van Riper, 178.

106　*Time*, August 17, 1998.

BIBLIOGRAPHY

Bond, Peter. *Heroes in Space: From Gagarin to Challenger.* New York: Basil Blackwell, 1987.

Cassutt, Michael. *Who's Who in Space.* Boston: G. K. Hall, 1987.

Collins, Michael. *Carrying the Fire: An Astronaut's Journey.* New York: Farrar, Straus and Giroux, 1974.

Politics in America 1998: The 105th Congress. Washington, D.C.: Congressional Quarterly Press, 1997.

Slayton, Donald K. with Michael Cassutt. *Deke! U.S. Manned Space: From Mercury to the Shuttle.* New York: Tom Doherty Associates, Inc., 1994.

Time, August 17, 1998.

Van Riper, Frank. *Glenn: The Astronaut Who Would Be President.* New York: Empire Books, 1983.

Wolfe, Tom. *The Right Stuff.* New York: Farrar, Straus and Giroux, 1979.

INDEX

OTHER TITLES IN LERNER'S BIOGRAPHY® SERIES:

Arthur Ashe
Christopher Reeve
Legends of Dracula
Louisa May Alcott
Madeleine Albright
Maya Angelou

Mother Teresa
Nelson Mandela
Princess Diana
Rosie O'Donnell
Women in Space

About the Author

Tom Streissguth is the author of more than thirty nonfiction books for young readers. He has written books on history and geography, and biographies on a wide range of subjects for Lerner's Biography® series. He lives in Florida, where he continues to write more books and screenplays.

Photo Acknowledgments

Official Navy Photo provided courtesy of the National Museum of Naval Aviation, pp. 6, 14; UPI/Corbis-Bettmann, pp. 2, 8, 18, 22 (left), 24, 28, 46, 56, 70, 72, 73, 77, 80, 88, 92; Corbis-Bettmann, p. 9; Seth Poppel Yearbook Archives, pp. 10, 11 (both), 12; US Air Force Museum, p. 14; Smithsonian Institution #80508A.C., p. 22 (right); AP/Wide World Photos, pp. 29, 37, 40, 41, 49, 66, 68, 74, 76, 79, 82, 95, 97; Lambert/Archive Photos, p. 34; Archive Photos, pp. 44; National Aeronautics and Space Administration (NASA), pp. 48, 50, 52, 53, 55, 58, 61, 91, 100, 102, 103, 105; Corbis/UPI-Bettmann, p. 71; UWE WALZ/Corbis, pp. 81, 93; the Ohio Historical Society # P339/11/3, p. 87; Reuters/Bruce Young/Archive Photos, p. 94; Reuters/Mike Segar/Archive Photos, p. 107.

Cover photos
Hardcover: front, NASA; back: AP/Wide World Photos
Softcover: front, UPI/Corbis-Bettmann; back, NASA